KNOW
THE FACTS

RELATIONSHIPS

Sarah Medina

WAYLAND

First published in 2008
by Wayland

Copyright © Wayland 2008

Wayland
338 Euston Road
London NW1 3BH

Wayland Australia
Level 17/207 Kent Street
Sydney, NSW 2000

Series editor: Nicola Edwards
Consultant: David Ferguson
Designer: Rawshock Design
Picture researcher: Kathy Lockley

All pictures posed by models. The author and publisher would like to thank the models, and the following
for allowing their pictures to be reproduced in this publication: Bubbles Photolibrary/Alamy: 36; Corbis:
COVER, 9, 44; Fancy/Veer/Corbis: 34; Geoff A. Howard/Alamy: 43; moodboard/Corbis: 17; Stephen
Oliver/Alamy: 38; Photofusion Picture Library/Alamy: 22; Picture Partners/Alamy: 30; Charlie
Schuck/Stock This Way/Corbis: 4; Take 2 Productions/Brand X/Corbis: 15; Thinkstock/Corbis: 18;
Arthur Turner/Alamy: 31; Wishlist: 5-8, 11-14, 16, 19-21, 24-27, 29, 32, 33, 35, 39-42, 45; David Young-
Wolff/Alamy: 28

British Library Cataloguing in Publication Data
Medina, Sarah
   Relationships. - (Know the facts)
   1. Interpersonal relations –
   Juvenile literature
   I. Title
   302
ISBN: 978 0 7502 5383 3

Printed in China

Wayland is a division of Hachette Children's Books,
an Hachette Livre UK company.
www.hachettelivre.co.uk

CONTENTS

PART OF EVERYDAY LIFE

We all have parents or other caregivers, and perhaps we have brothers and sisters, too. We may have grandparents, aunts, uncles and cousins. Many people have step-parents, and perhaps they have step-brothers or step-sisters. As we go through life, we make friends with many different people. We also relate to others, such as teachers, shopkeepers or bus drivers, in our day-to-day lives. We have relationships with all these people.

Long and short, good and bad

Some relationships only last a short time; others last a lifetime. But all our relationships are important. Good relationships make us feel loved, happy and confident. Bad relationships can make us feel miserable, and can make life seem like really hard work.

Few people are actually taught about relationships, and about what makes relationships work or go wrong. Most of us learn as we go along. Sometimes, that can be easy but, at other times, it can be tricky. We — like everyone else — can get things wrong.

Family and friends

Our very first relationships are with our family. Just by living in a family, we pick up good relationship skills or bad ones, without even thinking about it. As we get older, we start to have relationships with people outside the family. If we have not learned good relationship skills from our parents or caregivers, it can be harder to enjoy positive relationships with friends, teachers and other people.

Good relationships with the members of our family provide a strong foundation for positive relationships with others.

Help yourself

Think about your relationships

It can be really useful to sit down and think about all the different relationships you have. Who are your family members? Who are your friends? Who else do you have a relationship with? Think about what your different relationships are like. Are they happy? Open? Honest? Respectful? Difficult? Horrible? Then think about what you want them to be like. You can learn ways to make your relationships better and stronger.

All our interactions with other people are relationships. No matter how brief or trivial they may seem, they are still important.

In this book, you will learn about what relationships are, and what makes a relationship good or bad. You will go on to look at relationships with different people – with parents, siblings, friends and others. You will discover what can go wrong with relationships, and learn ways to deal with difficult situations. By reading this book, you can help yourself to enjoy or to improve the relationships you have right now – as well as those you will have in the future.

HAVE YOUR SAY

"I love my nan – she always has time for me and I can tell her anything."

"My brother's really annoying – we fight all the time."

WHAT ARE RELATIONSHIPS?

No one goes through life without relationships. We all have relationships from the time we are born – with parents, siblings and other relatives, with friends and acquaintances, with teachers and people in the community – even with people we have never met, in Internet social networking sites. We may not know a lot of people, but we all know someone! And, just by knowing someone, we have a relationship with them.

When relationships go well, between brothers and sisters in a family, for example, it makes people feel happy and secure.

Our relationships with the people we know or meet are often quite different from each other. Family relationships, and some friendships, can be very intense. Other friendships – for example, with classmates or team mates – may be more casual. Relationships with people such as shopkeepers and school nurses may be very transient.

HAVE YOUR SAY

"I love my mate Katie. We do everything together! We hang out every day after school, and we talk about everything. We even swap clothes! I don't know what I'd do without her."

"I get on with most of the teachers at my school, but there are some who just seem to be in a bad mood all the time."

"I go round with a group of friends. I don't have a best friend."

Good relationships

In the best relationships, we can be honest and we feel accepted for who we are. Good relationships make us feel loved, respected, safe and supported. It is great when we can talk openly to people about what we think and feel, and when people listen to us with care. This makes us feel equal – and important. Good relationships can make us feel confident to try new things, to meet other people and to enjoy life to the full.

WHAT'S THE PROBLEM?

'My dad says that I have to do what he says, because he's an adult and I'm only a kid. Is this right? Isn't everyone equal?'

It is true that parents and some other people, such as teachers, have authority over young people in their care. They have a responsibility to make sure that you're OK. Even so, good relationships mean having respect for each other – and this is a way of showing equality. Your dad's views are important – but yours are, too.

A bullying relationship is very painful, not only physically, but emotionally, too.

Running into problems

No relationship is ever perfect and even the best relationships can run into problems. This is because everyone is an individual, and each person may have different beliefs and feelings that affect the relationship. Also, everyone has 'bad days', when they may feel grumpy or sad.

Ideally, all our relationships would be good – but this is not always the case. In bad relationships, one person may want to control the other person. They may have a bad temper. They may say and do things that are hurtful or abusive. They may be jealous and possessive.

FAMILY RELATIONSHIPS

Family relationships can be the best – and the hardest. People often say that we can choose our friends, but we cannot choose our family! Sometimes, family relationships need a lot of work. Everyone in a family is different, with different wants and needs. There are times when this can cause family members to clash with each other.

No matter what our family set-up is like, the relationships we have with our family members are vital to our well-being.

Families today

Families come in all shapes and sizes! A 'traditional' family usually means a married mother and father, with children. However, nowadays, families may look very different to this. Some families have unmarried parents. Some families are lone-parent families. In these families, children may live part of the time with one parent, and the rest of the time with the other.

Some people live in extended families. Others live in step-families, adoptive families or foster families.

Some children have parents who are the same sex. Some families are mixed race. In some families, neither parent, one parent or both parents may go out to work.

It's a Fact

In the UK in 2006, 12.1 million families had married parents, and 2.3 million families had unmarried parents. In the same year, there were 2.6 million lone-parent families.

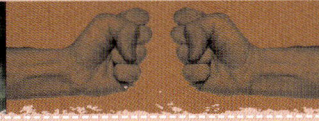

Different families, different ways

Every family has its own way of doing things. In some families, spending time together is important; 'family time' is when people talk to each other or work out any problems. In other families, people are very independent and do their own thing. Families have different rules, too. Some parents expect children to help with housework. Others believe that children should focus on study and play. In some families, parents set the rules. In others, decisions are made together by all family members.

Good family relationships are wonderful. They make people feel special and happy. Sadly, some families have problems that hurt young people (see pages 34-41). Every family brings different challenges, as well as joys. No matter what our families are like, we can usually find some good in them. Our families can be the best place we can go for love and support.

When families spend time together, it can open up the opportunity to talk about important issues in a safe, secure environment.

WHAT'S THE PROBLEM?

'My friend has loads of problems with her family. They argue a lot, and she's really unhappy. What can I say to her?'

It's sad that your friend is unhappy at home. Perhaps she could sit down with her family and tell them calmly and openly about how she feels. She could say that sitting down together and sorting things out will stop things turning into arguments. Everyone in a family needs to love and care for each other, and help each other out.

Parents

Parents and other caregivers have a legal responsibility to look after their children until they turn 18. They provide food, clothing and shelter, as well as emotional support and practical help. Some parents help with their children's education, and provide opportunities to enjoy activities such as dance or sport. It is worth thinking about – and appreciating – the good things our parents do for us.

Perfect parents?

Children and parents can have a lot of fun together. Good relationships with parents can be very loving and supportive. Many children would rather turn to their parents for help than talk to their friends.

Being a parent is not always easy – and, sometimes, parents get things wrong.

However, most parents try to do their very best for their children. Even though parents may not be perfect, most children feel loved and cared for at home.

Rules, rules, rules!

In many families, parents set house rules. Perhaps they say that their child cannot hang out with a particular friend or go to a particular place. They may expect their children to do jobs around the house, such as cleaning their room or clearing up after a meal. Some young people resent these rules, and think they are pointless. House rules can cause problems between parents and their children.

It can help to think about why parents set rules. Perhaps they worry that a particular friend might get their child into trouble. They may see danger in places that young

HAVE YOUR SAY

"My mum takes me to singing lessons every week, and to concerts and rehearsals, too. She's always there to help me."

"If I'm worried about something, talking to my mum about it always makes me feel better."

"My dad has to travel a lot with his job, so I don't see him much during the week."

"My parents get cross with me when my bedroom's in a mess."

Most parents and caregivers try to do their best to love, help and support their children.

people think are safe. Some house rules are about protecting children from harm. Other rules help everyone to live together happily and to respect each other. If housework is shared, this means that everyone has some time free to do other, more enjoyable, things. If one family member has to do all the work, it is unfair.

If children do not agree with a house rule, it can help to talk to their parents about it. By talking and listening to each other with care, it is possible to work things out.

Help yourself

Communication is key

Good communication is about listening as much as talking. If you need to talk to your parents about a problem, speak calmly and quietly. Don't shout! Listen to what your parents have to say, and try to see things from their point of view, too. Sometimes, the words people use get in the way of what they really want to say, so always try to listen to the meaning, as well as the words.

Having different interests from our siblings does not mean that we cannot be close and enjoy spending time together.

Brothers and sisters

People may complain at times about their brothers and sisters — but siblings can have a very special bond. They can be true friends. Because siblings live in the same family, they share a lot of experiences. Because of this, they can understand — and help and support — each other in ways that no one else can.

It's a Fact

- At least 80 per cent of people in the UK have at least one brother or sister.

Even though siblings grow up in the same family, they may be very different. They may have different personalities, and enjoy different activities. They may like different food, music, games or books. But being different does not mean that siblings cannot get along. No one is ever the same, and it is good to recognize and accept differences between people. Life would be very boring if everyone were identical!

In some families, siblings do find it hard to get on with each other. This is called sibling rivalry, and it is perfectly normal. Brothers and sisters often grow out of sibling rivalry over time. They can also learn ways to handle it and to make things better (see pages 14-15).

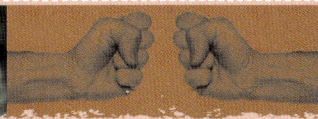

Everyone's special

Sometimes, parents may have different expectations of their different children. The eldest child may have to be responsible and look after younger siblings. The youngest child may be a little over-protected and perhaps a little spoiled. Parents sometimes do not want their youngest child to grow up too quickly. Middle children may do things to get attention, because they are not so sure of where they 'fit in'. But it is important to remember that everyone in the family is loved – and special.

Having brothers and sisters can be really great. People can feel proud of their siblings, and really like and love them. Siblings can look out for us, and help, protect and support us. Rather than comparing ourselves with our siblings, respecting our differences and focusing on our own good points is a healthier thing to do. Siblings can be our best friends.

Brothers and sisters have a special bond, which can last a lifetime.

HAVE YOUR SAY

"My older sister and I go to the same school. I'm glad she's there – I know she'd look out for me if I had a problem or if someone started trying to bully me."

Sibling rivalry

Brothers and sisters may compare themselves with each other, and find it hard to get along with each other. They may argue a lot, call each other names or tease each other. They may even hit each other. These displays of sibling rivalry can make people feel really miserable.

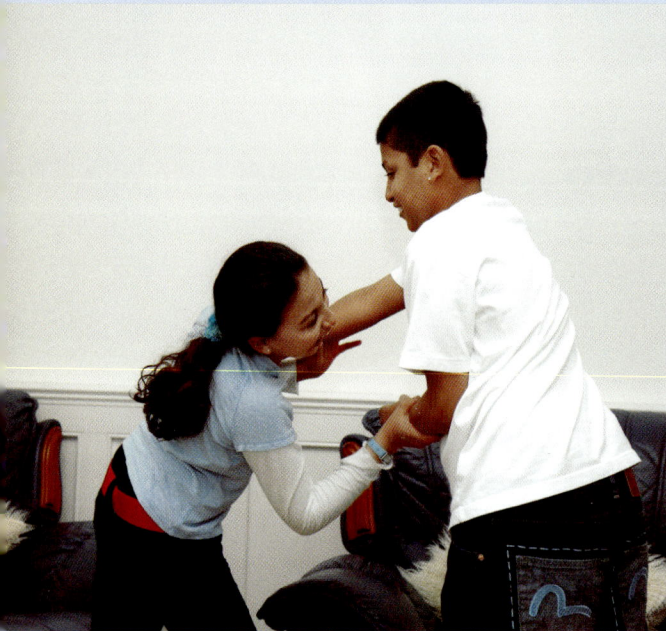

It is normal for siblings to argue at times, but abuse and violence are not normal – and not acceptable.

Sometimes, sibling rivalry is about competing for parents' attention. If a parent spends a lot of time with one child, such as a new baby, other children may feel left out. Sometimes, siblings get annoyed because their parents seem to compare them. Parents may say unhelpful things, such as 'Glen is the intelligent one' and 'Elizabeth tries hard'. This may cause brothers and sisters to believe that parents love their sibling more than them. This is hardly ever true – but the feeling can be very strong.

Sibling rivalry is sometimes about personal space. It can be frustrating if a brother or sister goes into your room or borrows your things without asking. It can be upsetting, too, if a sibling refuses to share their belongings with you. Some brothers and sisters, especially if they are older, like to feel more powerful than their siblings. They may tease and torment them, because this makes them feel stronger and in control.

HAVE YOUR SAY

"My sister Anna likes cooking, so she always helps mum in the kitchen. It's really annoying, because mum always tells people how good she is. But it's just that Anna enjoys it!"

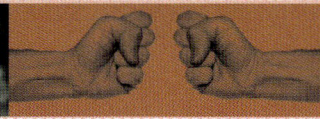

Who better to enjoy fun times with than a brother or sister who really knows and loves you?

You find your sister reading your personal diary, which you had hidden in a box under your bed. Do you:

a) Shout at her and tell her you hate her.

b) Go into her room and look through all her stuff when she's out.

c) Tell her calmly that you feel upset that she has read your diary, because it is private. Say that you respect her belongings – and she should respect yours, too.

Turn to page 47 for the answers.

Sibling rivalry might be worse at some times than others. If someone is having trouble with their parents or friends, or at school, they may be more likely to take out their problems on their brother or sister. This is often because they know that their sibling will always love them no matter what they do.

Sibling rivalry can be hard – but it can be a good way to learn to get along with other people. If siblings accept their differences, and remember to respect each other, the rivalry can melt away. And sibling rivalry does not last forever. The bond between siblings is very strong. We can have some of the best relationships in our lives with the people we grow up with.

When families break up

Sadly, family relationships can go wrong. Sometimes, parents decide that they cannot live together anymore. Perhaps they have been arguing a lot, or they have fallen out of love. They may decide to separate, and then get a divorce. This can be very difficult for all the family, and especially for young people.

A confusion of feelings

Children whose parents separate often worry a great deal. They may be anxious about what is going to happen to them – and to their mum and dad. They may be scared that they will have to move to a new home, school or town. They may feel angry at their parents for breaking up the family.

Most children feel very sad when parents decide to separate. Some feel guilty, because they think that the break-up is their fault. Some children feel relieved, especially if there were a lot of arguments at home. This can make them feel guilty, too. It is very important to remember that children are never the cause of family break-up.

When families break up, relationships are bound to change. Because tensions are reduced, they may well change for the better.

Moving on

Family break-up is very painful. It may not seem like it at first, but things can – and do – improve, over time. Until that happens, children need to do whatever they can to feel better. If possible, they should talk to

It's a Fact

- In the UK, it is predicted that more than 40 per cent of marriages will end in divorce.

parents about how they feel. Parents may not love each other anymore – but they still love their children, and they can give them the help and support they need.

Step-families

After getting divorced, many parents meet and fall in love with someone new. They may even decide to get married again. Young people may find that they now belong to a step-family. It can take time to get used to living with step-parents and step-siblings. Lots of patience – and time – is needed before things settle down. A step-family will always be different to our first family – but it can be just as happy and successful.

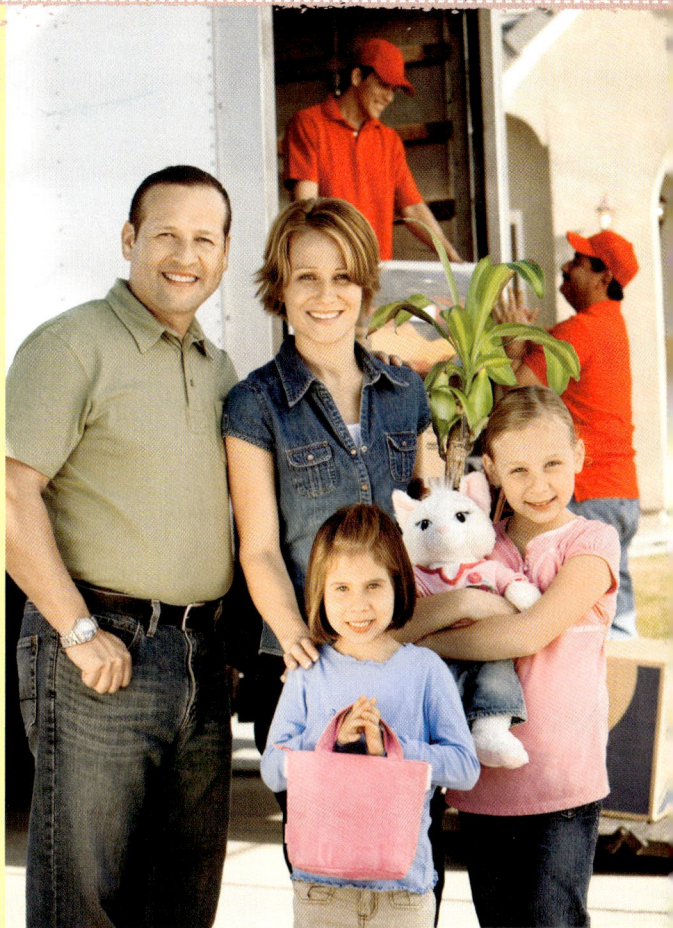

Living in a step-family may not always be easy, but step-families today usually go on to form strong and caring relationships.

Help yourself

Don't keep it to yourself

It can be very hard when parents separate. Whatever you do, try not to lock your feelings in. If you can, talk to your mum and dad, or to another relative or trusted friend.

Some children get their feelings out by playing music loudly and dancing, or by playing sport. Writing things down, or painting, can help, too. Remember, whatever you are feeing is normal – and OK. And you will not always feel this way.

HAVE YOUR SAY

"When my mum and dad were getting divorced I found it really hard. I talked to my friend Kate about it. Her parents split up last year, so she understood how I was feeling. That helped me a lot."

RELATIONSHIPS WITH FRIENDS

A friend is someone we get along well with and choose to spend time with. People have lots of friends throughout their lives. Even babies can have friends! Some friendships last for years – even a lifetime. Others end after just a few weeks or months. No matter how long a friendship lasts, our friends are really important.

Different types of friendship

Some people have 'best' friends, who they are especially close to. People can usually talk to their best friend about their deepest thoughts and feelings. Best friends understand us and care for us in a special way. People sometimes have different best friends as they go through different stages of their life.

Some people, especially boys, have groups of friends, rather than one or two close friends. Being part of a group of friends can be great. It makes people feel part of

something important. Friends in a group may dress in a similar way to each other. They may listen to the same music and enjoy the same activities, such as sport.

Activities we enjoy can be even more fun if they are shared with good friends.

WHAT'S THE PROBLEM?

I've never had a best friend. Is there something wrong with me?

No, there is nothing wrong with you at all! Not everyone has – or wants to have – a best friend. Some people prefer to hang out with a variety of different people. Just enjoy the friendships you have!

Ups and downs

Friends can teach us important life skills. They can teach us how to get on with people who are different from us, and about being caring and loyal. We often have a lot of fun with our friends, but friendships are not always perfect. Some people try to make their friends do things they do not want to do. This is negative peer pressure, and it can be very hard to deal with (see pages 34-35).

Even good friends can hurt each other's feelings. Because we are all different, friends may disagree about things they believe or want to do. People may be a little selfish or tactless at times, and forget that what they say or do might upset a friend.

Problems with friends can often be resolved by talking them over. And, when friends get over problems, their friendship can grow even stronger.

Sometimes, we cannot work out a friendship problem, and we may have to be prepared simply to put the problem behind us and move on.

HAVE YOUR SAY

"My mate said he'd come and play football with me in the park, but he didn't turn up. Later, I found out he'd gone to someone else's house to watch a DVD. It was really annoying."

friend, a good friend does not try to stop them. Sometimes, people just want to have time alone, too. A good friend respects this and gives their friend the space they need.

Sharing and caring

Good friends always care about their friend's feelings and problems. They try to help out as much as they can – in the right way. They may ask their friend if they want to talk about things – but they do not push them. They respect their friend's right not to talk.

A good friend can help his friend by helping to take his mind off his problems, even for a short while.

What makes a good friend?

People may know lots of people, and even have lots of friends. But good friends are really special. A good friend is someone who is there for us, no matter what. Good friends listen to us and respect us. They help and support us if we have a problem. Good friends really appreciate each other, and they let each other know that they like and care about each other.

A good friend does not get jealous or do anything to hurt their friend. If someone wants to spend time with family or another

What Would you do?

You want to go out with a new friend from school, but your best friend gets really jealous. Do you:

a) Tell your best friend that you really like them and don't want to hurt their feelings, but you want to spend a bit of time alone with your new friend. Say you can all go out together another time.

b) Get fed up and tell your friend that what you do is none of their business.

c) Pull out of seeing your new friend; it's too much hassle.

Turn to page 47 for the answers.

Good friends know when to speak – and when to listen. A listening ear may be all that somebody needs to work out how to deal with an issue.

If a friend does share her problems, good friends listen quietly and carefully. They allow their friend to be upset and cry, if this is what she needs. They do not tell the friend what she should do. Instead, they ask what their friend needs, and how they can help. If the problem is serious, and if their friend wants this, they could talk to a trusted adult and get further help.

Sometimes, people just need to be distracted from their problems. Good friends know when to do this. They invite their friend to do something fun with them, that they will both enjoy. Kicking a ball in the garden or park can be a good way to help people to forget their worries or let off steam.

It is not always easy to be a good friend, especially if we are busy or worried. But we can all learn and practise ways to be the best friend we can to the people we care about.

HAVE YOUR SAY

"I had a bit of a row with my sister, and it upset me a lot for a while. I felt really miserable. My friend Jasmin asked me round to her house. We played a game and watched a film, and it was really great. She didn't force me to talk about things, but I felt so much better after seeing her."

How to make friends

Making friends may seem easy – but it can actually be quite hard. Sometimes, people just click, and making friends is no trouble at all. At other times, making friends can seem scary – and a bit like hard work! Fortunately, we can all learn skills to help us to make new friends.

Help yourself

Don't be in a rush

Remember – it's much easier to make just one new friend at a time. If you want lots of friends, the rest can follow later!

Finding friends

Everyone is different. Some people are outgoing and naturally friendly. They are not afraid to talk to people they do not know. Other people are quiet and reserved. They may be shy and worried about talking to somebody new, especially if they have moved to a new school or town. This can make it harder for them to make new friends. Some people lack self-confidence. They may believe that no one will like them. But this is never true – everyone can be fun to be with and a good friend to someone else.

A good way to make new friends is to go to a group activity, such as a drama group or a sports team. This might be at school or in the community. By joining a group, we already know that there are people who share the same interests as us. This is a great starting point for friendship!

Smile, please!

You may feel nervous, or even a little scared about meeting new people, but it really helps to make an effort to be open and friendly. Smiling, saying 'Hello' and telling people your name is a safe way to break the ice. If you smile at people, they'll think that you are approachable and easy to talk to. This will make them want to spend some time getting to know you.

We do not have to be exciting or fascinating to make new friends. Being nice – and interested in others – is enough! We can start a conversation with someone just by talking about something that is happening around us. Asking people questions and listening to their answers is good, too. Great friendships can grow from these small steps.

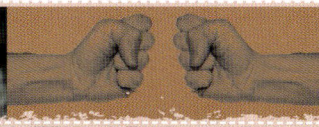

If you are nervous about making new friends, joining a group or club, such as a drama group or sports club, is one of the easiest ways to meet new people.

Help yourself

Be a good listener

Good listening skills can help you to make new friends! Always look at the person who is speaking, and show them you are listening, perhaps by nodding here and there. Don't interrupt them but, when you can, ask them questions to find out more. Repeating what they have said in your own words shows them that you are really interested in them.

How to keep a friend

Everyone needs someone to care about and to care about them. Friends are important to almost everyone. No one likes to feel lonely. People need friends to enjoy happy times with – and to share worries with, too. Friendship can make life feel good!

When we have a good friend, we should never take them for granted. We should treat our friends as we would like to be treated ourselves. If someone treats us unfairly or unkindly, it is hurtful. If we do this to other people, it is hurtful to them, too.

Being kind, caring and respectful are important qualities that will help a friendship to last. Being able to compromise is good, too. No one wants to have to do what someone else wants all the time. People like to have friends who are fun to be with, who do not moan all the time, and who are good at thinking of things to do.

People also need friends who will support and help them when they need it.

When friends have an argument, it can be

Having fun together is a great way to keep a friendship going strong.

HAVE YOUR SAY

"I like hanging out with my mates Danny and Jamie. They've always got loads of ideas of what to do – we have a real laugh."

"I was friends for ages with a girl in my class, then she suddenly joined another group and started saying I was boring. I was really upset."

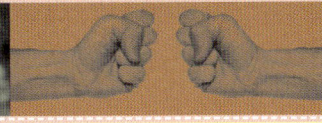

upsetting. If we argue, we should try not to say hurtful things to our friends. We should try to see things from their point of view, as well as our own. This will help the argument to pass more quickly. Arguments do not have to mean the end of a friendship.

Old and new

We all make new friends as we go through life. Perhaps there is a new person at school, who we get on really well with. Having different friends is interesting and enjoyable. But people should not reject their 'old' friends when they make a new friend. It is possible to have old friends and new friends at the same time. Sometimes, we may want to see just one friend, and that is fine. At other times, it is fun to go out with all our friends – old and new together.

WHAT'S THE PROBLEM?

'I've got a new friend, but she doesn't ever want to go out with my other friends. What should I do?'

It could be that your new friend feels shy or nervous about meeting your other friends. She may worry that they won't like her. You could start out by inviting just one other friend to do something with you both. Later, she might feel happier and more confident to hang out in a bigger group.

It's great to have different friends, and it's especially satisfying when all our friends get along together.

School friends

As we go through school, we meet lots of different people. There are too many people at school for them all to be our friends, so most people have their own 'circle' of friends. Some of these may be more casual friends, who we chat to in class or in the school playground. Others become closer friends. Many people have a school friend who becomes their best friend, too.

School friends are important. Before we go to school, most of our relationships are with our family. When we go to school, we learn to interact with all sorts of different people. This can be sometimes be difficult, especially if people seem very different from us. But having good school friends helps us to enjoy and get the most out of our school years. Good school friends are not only fun to be with at break times, but they can also help us with our schoolwork and be there for us if we have a problem.

Help yourself

Be friendly!

When someone joins a new school, they often feel nervous – and even a little bit scared. You can help them by talking to them and making them feel welcome. You can introduce them to your other friends, too.

Them and us

Sometimes, young people at school form a clique. This is a group of friends that leave other people out on purpose. Usually, one

People who are not accepted by a clique can feel very isolated and rejected.

or two people in the clique decide who can join the clique and who cannot. People who do not look, act or dress in the 'right way' are often left out. This can make them feel very lonely.

Being part of a clique often makes people feel special, 'cool' and popular. But cliques are not always healthy. Sometimes, people in cliques are mean to people on the 'outside'. Cliques can close down the possibility of other, rewarding friendships. Being in a clique can change people, too. Someone might be really nice on their own, but they act differently in the clique, because they want to fit in. Being in a clique can stop us from being ourselves.

We do not have to be part of a clique to have good friends at school. If we are in a clique, we have to look and act as the rest of the clique does. It is far better to be true to ourselves. Then we can choose the people we want to be friends with, whenever we want to.

We can be good friends with anyone we like – even if there is an age gap between us.

HAVE YOUR SAY

"I was in a clique for a while – but, in the end, I didn't like it. There was this other girl I wanted to be friends with, but no one in the clique wanted to know her."

"I'm not interested in being part of a clique. I think people only join them because they're not confident enough to make their own friends."

OTHER RELATIONSHIPS

Throughout our lives, we meet hundreds, if not thousands, of different people – at school, at work and in our community. We have relationships with teachers, sports or music coaches, doctors and dentists. As we get older, we go out with different boyfriends or girlfriends. We meet all sorts of people when we are out and about, such as school crossing patrol officers, shopkeepers and bus drivers. Some people chat to other people in Internet chatrooms or on social networking sites, even though they have never met them. These are all different kinds of relationships – even though they may be quite transient.

We may not spend a long time with some of the people we meet in a day, but these relationships are important, too.

Teachers

Teachers are an important part of people's lives throughout school. Some teachers are interesting and fun – and very easy to like. Some are more serious and even quite strict. Like everyone, every teacher has his or her unique personality.

HAVE YOUR SAY

"My English teacher is the best! He always has time to talk to me and to help with problems with my homework. He's a really patient person."

People cannot choose their teachers. Just as people like some people more than others, they will also like some teachers more than others. It is important to be able to get used to – and get along with – the different teachers we meet throughout school. Learning to interact with different kinds of people is a great life skill. Getting on well with teachers also makes school life more enjoyable – and helps people to achieve more.

Teachers need young people to pay attention in class, and to be respectful and polite. They want students to try to learn as much as they can. Young people need teachers who are on their side, who respect them and try to help them learn.

Thinking about each other's needs can help pupils and their teachers to have the kind of good relationship they both deserve.

What Would you do?

You have a teacher you don't get along with very well. Do you:

a) Talk about the teacher to your friends, saying how awful they are and how much you dislike them.
b) Ask to talk to your teacher after class, and tell them that you really want to do well in their subject and that you need their help.
c) Try to make the teacher's life as hard as possible by messing around in lessons.

Turn to page 47 for the answers.

Teachers and students can enjoy a healthy, positive relationship with each other, which benefits both.

Feeling attracted to another person is a normal and healthy part of growing up.

Boyfriends and girlfriends

As children get older, they find that their bodies change as they go through the process of puberty. How they feel and what they think starts to change, too. They may find that they start to be interested in having a girlfriend or boyfriend. Their feelings towards someone who has been 'just' a friend may start to change.

As children, we often have both girls and boys as friends. It can sometimes come as a surprise when we suddenly find that we want more than 'just friendship' with someone. Our feelings can be quite strong. We might get butterflies in our stomach whenever we see the person we like. We may blush. Some people get tongue-tied when the person they like talks to them. This is perfectly natural. It happens to everyone – and everyone gets past it.

Help yourself

Be yourself

It is completely normal to be a little nervous when you have a boyfriend or girlfriend for the first time. But don't be too nervous! Remember, don't try to change who you are just to impress the other person. Just be yourself – and have fun!

The dating game

The idea of going on a date can seem daunting. But a date is simply when two people do something interesting and fun together that they both enjoy, such as going to the cinema or going for a walk in a park. Whatever we do, we should always make sure we are safe and comfortable when we go on a date. Telling our parents where we are going and when we will be home is always sensible.

Sometimes, young people feel under pressure to take part in sexual activity when they are on a date. We are all surrounded by sexual images, in adverts and TV programmes, and these can make sex seem normal, fun and cool. However, sexual activity is not as common as these images make out. And no one should ever feel pressurized into sexual activity before they are ready.

Dating can be fun – but there is no hurry to start the dating game! People can have a lot of fun with friends, without taking it a step further. There is plenty of time to have a boyfriend or girlfriend. It is better not to rush into anything too quickly.

It can be just as much fun to spend time with someone who is 'just' a friend than with a boyfriend or girlfriend.

It's a Fact

- In the UK, 25 per cent of young women and 30 per cent of young men under the age of 16 have had sex.

Out and about

We come across lots of different people when we are out and about – either on a day-to-day basis, or just occasionally. Our relationships with these people is often very casual. If we go to a shop, we interact with the shopkeeper. If we go to the library, we talk to a librarian. Some people catch the bus to school, and they may talk to the bus driver – even just to say 'Hello'. Young people often enjoy using the Internet, and they may use chatrooms or social networking sites to 'talk' to other people with the same interests as them.

Many people think that these kinds of casual relationships do not matter. But the way we interact with other people is always

Taking the time to talk to other people adds interest and pleasure to the day.

HAVE YOUR SAY

"When I got the bus to town, I didn't have any small change to buy my ticket. The bus driver was horrible to me – he made me feel really embarrassed, in front of all the other people. I was meeting my friend, but all I could think about was what he said. It ruined everything."

important. If people ignore us or say something rude to us, it can make us feel sad and unsettled. If we do the same to them, it can spoil their day, too.

Everyone can learn to be polite to other people. Being polite does not just mean saying 'Please' and 'Thank you' – although this is important, too. It means remembering that everyone has their own thoughts, feelings and problems – and respecting this. If we make an effort to smile and be nice to people, our casual relationships can actually be enjoyable.

Safety first

Although it is good to be polite to people we do not know, safety should always come first. Young people should never give out their personal details, such as their address or phone number, to someone they do not know well – no matter how friendly the person seems. And people should always go out with family members or friends, so they do not put themselves in danger.

Cyber-buddies may seem like good friends – but nothing can replace the contact we enjoy with the 'real-life' friends we normally hang out with.

WHAT'S THE PROBLEM?

'I've been chatting to someone on the Internet, and they've asked me to meet up with them after school. What should I do?'

People you meet on the Internet might seem really nice and good fun – and maybe you're tempted to see them. But you should never, ever meet up with anyone you talk to online without taking an adult you trust, such as your mum or dad, with you. Sometimes, adults who want to abuse children use the Internet to pretend to be friends with young people. It is not worth the risk.

HANDLING RELATIONSHIP PROBLEMS

Good relationships are fantastic – they make us feel strong, confident and happy. In good relationships, people respect each other and know how to communicate with each other to overcome any problems. Sadly, not all relationships are good. Peer pressure, bullying, abuse and serious conflict can all occur in bad relationships. These problems can be very damaging – and even dangerous. It is important to know how to deal with these types of relationship problems.

Resisting peer pressure can be hard, but it is better to stick to your own views than follow someone else's.

Peer pressure

Peer pressure is when a friend tries to persuade us to do something we do not want to do. Sometimes, peer pressure is positive. A good friend may encourage us to study harder, or to take up a hobby or sport, for example. But peer pressure is often negative. Friends may try to get us to do things we are not comfortable with, such as trying drugs or having sex.

It can be hard to stand up to peer pressure. But when people are pushed into doing something they do not want to do, it always makes them feel bad – and it can be

HAVE YOUR SAY

"I didn't want to go to the party because it was at someone's house who I didn't know – but my so-called mates kept laughing at me, saying I was scared and stupid. I had to lie to my mum to get out of the house. Everyone got really drunk at the party – including me. I felt so sick the day after. I wish I'd never gone."

dangerous. It is important to be clear about what we think and feel about different things. If someone tries to make us go against our views, we can tell someone we trust, such as our parents. They can help us stick to what we know is right.

People can help to avoid negative peer pressure by choosing their friends carefully. Good friends do not normally put their friends under pressure. We should not be afraid to change our friends, if necessary.

Remember – no one has the right to force us to do something we do not want to do. Real friends accept us for who we are, and always respect our views and decisions.

What Would you do? ?

A lot of your friends smoke, and they want you to smoke, too. Do you:

a) Say 'No, thanks. I don't like smoking, it's bad for you, and it's expensive, too.'
b) Get angry and tell them they're stupid for smoking.
c) Smoke one cigarette, just to shut them up.

Turn to page 47 for the answers.

The things we do and what we believe in are a large part of our identity. We are each unique, and we do not need to follow the crowd.

Bullying

Bullying is when someone hurts another person, either with words or with physical violence. Young people may be bullies, but adults can bully others, too. Sadly, bullying is a common relationship problem. Most people know someone who has been bullied at some point in their lives.

Bullies always want to be in control. They may do this by threatening, insulting or teasing their victims. This is called emotional bullying. They may become physically violent, damaging their victims' belongings, or hitting or kicking them. Young people sometimes bully others by taking their friends away from them. Some people use cyber-bullying to torment their victims. They may send insulting texts or emails, or post nasty messages on Internet social networking sites.

Being bullied is a frightening experience. Bullies can make their victims feel so bad that they lose all their self-esteem, and this can lead to depression.

All sorts of people can bully others. People who bully us are often young people at school. Our brothers, sisters, parents or teachers can bully us, too. Sometimes, people are bullied by strangers when they go out. Bullying can even happen to adults at work.

Help yourself

Beating the bullies

If you are being bullied, follow these tips to help you stay safe.

Try to travel to places with friends. There is safety in numbers, and a bully is much less likely to pick on you if you are not alone.

If possible, try to avoid going to places where you know the bully goes.

In a bullying situation, do not fight back. This almost always makes this worse, and it can be dangerous. Walk away – and get help as soon as you can from someone you trust.

Why bully?

People become bullies for lots of different reasons. They may feel jealous of the people they pick on. They may not like people who do not look or act like them. Some bullies have low self-esteem. Bullying makes them feel stronger, more important or more popular. Whatever the reasons for bullying, there is no excuse for it. And, no matter what bullies say, bullying is never the victim's fault. Bullying hurts – and it is wrong.

Getting help

It can be hard to deal with bullying without support from others. Victims of bullying can feel very alone – but there is always someone who cares for us who can help us. People who are being bullied should never keep the bullying a secret. Speaking out to a trusted adult is the best thing they can do. It can be the first step to ending the misery of bullying.

A friend in need

Friends can be very important to victims of bullying. By showing that we care about someone who is being bullied, it may make a bully think twice about bullying that person. And, because there is safety in numbers, spending time with the victim may help to keep them safe.

Abuse

Abuse is cruel and hurtful treatment of another person. Abuse can happen anywhere – at home, at school or in the community. It can be carried out by just about anyone – such as parents, siblings and friends. Even though someone is meant to love us and care for us, it does not always mean that they do.

It's a Fact

- According to the World Health Organization, approximately 40 million children in all parts of the world suffer child abuse each year.

Types of abuse

Emotional abuse is when someone hurts or damages someone's feelings by shouting at them, insulting them or making fun of them. Physical abuse is an attack on someone's body. Physical abusers may hit, punch, kick, burn or poison their victims. Sexual abuse is when someone forces somebody to engage in sexual activity. It is terrifying, and can be very dangerous, too.

Abuse is a terrible thing. It often ruins people's lives and their relationships with other people. People who have been abused can find it hard to trust other people for many years. They may lose their self-confidence and feel really bad about themselves.

Physical abuse is the most visible form of abuse, but emotional and sexual abuse are equally painful and damaging.

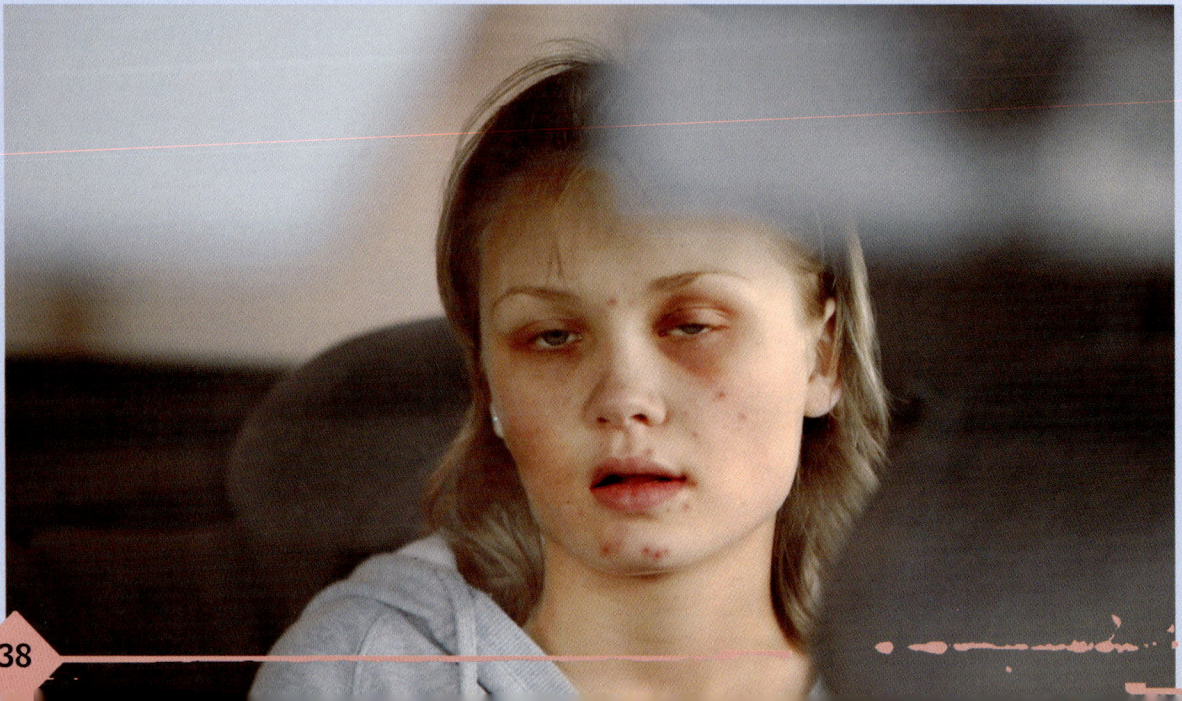

Speak out

If someone is abusing you, try to stay away from the abuser, as much as you possibly can. Always trust yourself – if something does not feel right, it is not right. Never blame yourself for the abuse. Abuse is never your fault. And don't ever feel ashamed to talk to someone you trust about the abuse. Speaking out is the very best thing you can do.

It can be hard for people to realize that they are being abused, especially if the abuser is someone close to them, who should love and care for them. Some victims of abuse have been abused for so long that they think the abuse is normal. Some abusers tell their victim that they are treating them in a particular way because they love them. This is never true. Abuse is all about power and control – and it is never part of a good, healthy relationship.

Getting help

Victims of abuse can feel very lonely. They may think that no one can help them. But everyone has someone who cares about them – such as a relative, teacher, doctor or friend. No matter how hard it may seem, victims of abuse really need to talk to someone they trust – if possible, an adult – in order to bring the abuse to an end. No one has to suffer abuse alone. Abuse can – and should – be stopped.

If you feel unable to talk to a family member or a friend about abuse, make an appointment to see your doctor or school nurse. They will be able to help you.

Conflict and arguments

It can be upsetting when conflict happens in a relationship with a family member or a friend. Conflict is when people disagree about something. It can lead to arguments, when people shout at each other.

Conflict hurts, and it can damage relationships permanently if it is left unresolved.

Feeling angry

When there is conflict, people may feel angry. Anger is one of many feelings people have, such as love, sadness and worry. It is OK to feel angry – but it is never OK to hurt anyone else with our anger.

Help yourself

Take your time

If you feel angry, or if someone is angry with you, it can really help to wait for a while before you say anything. Some people simply count to ten in their mind. This gives them time to clear their thoughts, and helps them to avoid saying something they might regret later.

Handling conflict

Some conflicts are about small things. It can be better, at times, just to let these problems go and not to make them into something bigger. Bigger conflicts usually need to be dealt with. Ignoring serious conflict can make people feel angry inside, and damage their relationship over time. The best way to handle conflict is to negotiate with the other person.

Negotiation is all about trying to find a way to agree with someone else. It involves calmly saying what we think, and listening carefully to what the other person has to say, too. When people negotiate, they find out and understand what each other thinks and feels. They can then work out a way forward that is acceptable to both of them.

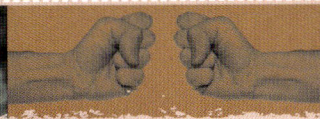

Negotiation is an effective way to handle conflict. It involves good communication skills - listening and speaking with respect.

I'm OK; you're OK

To negotiate well, it is useful to know how to be assertive. When people are passive, they do not speak up for themselves and they just let things happen. This can make them feel ignored and upset. When someone is aggressive, they force their views on someone else. They do not respect the other person's feelings or opinions. When someone is assertive, they respect their own needs – and also the needs of the other person. Assertive people understand that everyone is equal.

No one needs to be afraid of conflict. People can learn a lot from it. They can learn about themselves and about how to communicate better with other people. Handling conflict well can lead to better and stronger relationships.

HAVE YOUR SAY

"My brother took my football without asking me. I was really annoyed. But then I thought that he didn't mean to upset me. Plus, he didn't have his own football, and he always lends me his stuff if I want it. So I decided it wasn't worth arguing about."

THE KEY TO GOOD RELATIONSHIPS

Our relationships with parents or other caregivers, with brothers and sisters, and with uncles, aunts, cousins and grandparents, are some of the most important relationships we will ever have. Good family relationships help to create strong, healthy individuals. They make us feel safe, secure and loved. They also influence the relationships we have with other people throughout our lives.

Love, care and respect are key building blocks to developing happy, healthy relationships.

As time goes on, relationships with different family members change. This is perfectly normal. Throughout their lives, people learn lots of different things. The different stages of life make people grow and change. This is a great thing! It stops people – and life – becoming stuck and boring.

WHAT'S THE PROBLEM?

'My older sister doesn't want to spend time with me anymore. I feel really sad.'

As people get older, it is normal for them to develop different interests. Your sister might feel that she doesn't have anything in common with you at the moment. But don't worry – this will change. One day, you will be close again, as each of you grows and changes some more.

Talk – and listen!

We can all help to make sure that our family relationships stay strong and happy. Good communication is always important. This means not being afraid to say what we think and feel, and not being afraid to listen to what other people think and feel, either. Learning how to handle conflict helps to

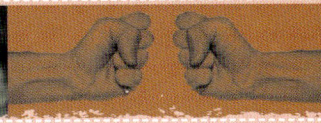

make sure that arguments do not get out of control (see page 40). If everyone in a family feels that they are equally important, they feel equally loved, too. Then relationships can grow stronger and stronger.

Building memories

Spending time as a family helps to make people feel closer. Some families enjoy playing games or watching films together. Others like to go on walks in the park or in the countryside. Family holidays can be good! Some families just like chatting to each other over a meal or before going to bed. Whatever families choose to do, they are building up happy memories for everyone to share and look back on over time.

It is important to really value our families, and to show love and care to every family member, every day. No matter what our family looks like, it is unique — and very special.

When family members enjoy outings and activities together, they not only enjoy themselves, but they form strong and lasting bonds with each other.

HAVE YOUR SAY

"I'm so lucky to have a family who's been there for me forever."

"I come from a big family and we do have our rows but we have a lot of laughs, too."

Great friends

Close friendships can be as important to us as family relationships. They can last a lifetime, and see us through all the good times and bad times we may go through. A really good, close friend is a gift from life. A good friend is someone we can laugh with – and someone we can talk to about anything. A good friend can grow up alongside us, sharing our experiences and understanding our feelings.

There for each other

Just as our friends are there for us, we can be there for them, too. Supporting someone who needs help is a great feeling. It can help us as much as them! Caring for someone else stops us from becoming selfish. Friends can teach us how to be a better person.

Friendships may start when we are young and remain strong as we go through all the different stages that life brings.

HAVE YOUR SAY

"I've known Liz since I was five – and now I'm nearly 50! Even though we've lived far away for most of our lives, we're still good friends. We've watched each other grow up, get married and have children. I hope we'll see get to enjoy each other's grandchildren one day, too!"

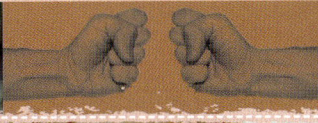

A friendship with someone you have known nearly all your life is easy and especially rewarding.

Good friends are the best! They are fun to spend time with. They can make us laugh and help us to feel positive about ourselves – and about life. Good friends have lots of good ideas about what to do, and listen to our ideas, too. They enjoy the activities their friend enjoys. They are not jealous – they can 'share' their friend with others. They are kind and thoughtful, willing to share their belongings and happy to help out. They always have a listening ear, and they respect their friend's thoughts and feelings.

A final word

Relationships really do make the world go round. Relationships can be the best part of people's lives. They can also be the most challenging. No one is the same as anyone else, and we all need to learn how to get on with each other. Getting to know another person really well can be exciting and fun. It can help us to grow and become better people. It is a process that never ends.

Help yourself

You can choose your friends

We meet many people in our life – and only some will be our friends. Always try to choose your friends carefully. If you get it right, someone might be your friend for life!

Glossary

abuse treating someone badly. Abuse can be emotional, physical or sexual

acquaintance someone you have met, but who you do not know well

adoptive family a family which has adopted a child. A child who is adopted is brought up legally by parents who did not give birth to the child

approachable friendly and easy to talk to

assertiveness confident behaviour that respects our own and other people's feelings and opinions

authority the ability to control someone or something

clique a group of people who leave other people out

community the people living in a particular place, such as a village or town

compromise to reach an agreement with someone about something, by taking their views into consideration, as well as your own

cyber-bullying bullying using mobile phones, email and the Internet

distracted to have your attention taken away from something

divorce the legal end of a marriage

equality the right to be treated in the same way as someone else

extended family family which may include grandparents, aunts, uncles and cousins, as well as parents and siblings

foster family a family which takes care of a child, either for a short or long time, without the adult member of the family being the child's legal parent

interact to communicate with someone

legal allowed by the law

lone-parent family a family in which only one parent looks after a child

mixed race a family in which parents come from a different religion or race

peer pressure the influence to behave in the same way as someone else who is of a similar age to you

personality the type of person you are, which is shown by the things you do and say

puberty a stage in life when a child grows and changes during the process of becoming an adult

relationship the way in which two or more people feel and behave towards each other

resent to be angry about something

reserved when someone does not easily show their feelings

separate to stop living together

sibling brother or sister

social networking site any Internet site where people post information and chat to each other, such as Facebook and MySpace

step-family a family that includes one natural parent living with another adult, and possibly with the other adult's children

transient lasting for a short time

Further information

BOOKS

Jane Bingham, Emotion and Relationships,
Heinemann Library, 2007

Ann McPherson and Aidan Macfarlane, The Truth:
Relationships, **OUP, 2004**

Odile Amblard, Friends Forever?: Understanding why
your friendships are so important, **HNA Books, 2008**

Angela Neustatter, Talking About Myself: My Family,
Franklin Watts, 2008

USEFUL ORGANIZATIONS AND WEBSITES

ChildLine

A confidential telephone service for vulnerable children
and teenagers to talk about their problems with a
trained counsellor. The website offers tips on how to
beat the bullies and stay safe.

www.childine.org.uk

Helpline number 0800 1111

There4Me

A website for 12- to 16-year-olds which has information
and message boards on a range of topics, such as
coping with depression and divorce in the family.

www.there4me.com

Young Minds

The website of a charity that promotes young people's
mental health.

www.youngminds.org.uk

WHAT WOULD YOU DO?

Page 15

a) Shouting at your sister will just make her feel defensive
   and angry, and it could make things worse.

b) You may feel like getting your own back on your sister, but
   do you really want to do something to her that you don't
   want her doing to you? Two wrongs never make a right!

c) It's great to get your feelings and thoughts across
   without getting angry. Letting your sister know that you
   respect her will help her to remember to respect you, too.

Page 20

a) Letting your best friend know that you care for them
   and want to include them later will help them to feel
   less jealous.

b) If your best friend thinks that you are annoyed with
   them, they will feel hurt. This not the way to deal with
   friends who are important to you.

c) If you back down about seeing your new friend, your best
   friend may put you under pressure every time you want
   to do something without them. A good friend should give
   you space to do different things, without getting jealous.

Page 29

a) Complaining to your friends won't change anything.

b) Letting your teacher know that you care about their
   subject is a good starting point. Asking for help shows
   the teacher that you want to do as well as you can.

c) If you don't pay attention in class, things can only get
   worse – your results, as well as your relationship with
   your teacher, will suffer.

Page 35

a) Staying calm and saying why you don't want to smoke gives
   the clear message that you won't give in to peer pressure.

b) Getting angry and insulting your friends might make
   things worse.

c) You don't need to do something just because your friends
   do it. Stick to what you believe in!

INDEX

Numbers in bold refer to illustrations.